A book of quotes to nurture teenage mindsets

A Guide to Building Resilience, Focus, and Confidence

Presented by Habit Mantra

notionpress.com

INDIA · SINGAPORE · MALAYSIA

ISBN
Paperback 979-8-89724-288-7
Hardcase 979-8-89906-807-2

To all the teens who dare to dream, challenge their limitations, and shape the world with their unique perspectives. May this book inspire you to embrace your journey, stay true to yourselves, and always keep growing. The future is yours to create.

Acknowledgement

This book is a heartfelt expression of gratitude to all those who have been part of our journey at Habit Mantra.

To Juhi, Rajanish, Akash, Madhuri and Isha—your dedication to curating meaningful content for teenagers and your unwavering belief in the power of words have been instrumental in making this book a reality. Thank you for your hard work, insight, and passion. Your contributions to the work that Habit Mantra does for teenagers are invaluable. From curating meaningful content to inspiring thoughtful discussions, your efforts have deeply enriched this book.

A special thank you to the incredible students who put their trust in us during our initial days: Surbhi, MJ, Shamirul, Mitul, Rithika, Kehkasha, Shruti, Adnan, Anushka, Kritika and many more. Your courage, determination, and hard work to improve your lives have inspired us deeply. You remind us every day why we do what we do and motivate us to continue striving to make a difference.

This book is a testament to the collective effort, belief, and shared vision of everyone involved. Thank you for being part of this journey.

Dear Reader,

Welcome to Teenage Mindsets. This book is a collection of wisdom, inspiration, and encouragement designed to resonate with the unique experiences of teens. Life as a teenager can feel like a whirlwind of emotions, choices, and discoveries. These quotes are here to remind you that you are not alone and that your journey is filled with endless possibilities.

Take your time with each quote. Reflect on its meaning, relate it to your life, and let it guide you toward growth, confidence, and resilience. Whether you're facing challenges, dreaming big, or simply looking for a spark of motivation, these words are for you. Remember, you are the author of your own story. May these pages inspire you to write it boldly, beautifully, and authentically.

Habit
Mantra

With love and hope,
Team Habit Mantra

LET'S BEGIN

"Workout because you love your body not because you hate it"

Unknown

Think about your body as a friend. If you had a friend who always supported you—like helping you climb stairs, play your favorite sport, or even just breathe—you wouldn't treat them badly, right? You'd want to take care of them and make them feel appreciated. **Exercise is one way of saying, "Thank you" to your body for everything it does for you.**

When you approach exercise with a positive attitude, it feels less like a chore and more like a way to show yourself some love and respect. It helps you stay consistent and enjoy the process more!

My rating ☆ ☆ ☆ ☆ ☆

My thoughts:

> "What you want and what you need aren't always the same"

Mandy Hale

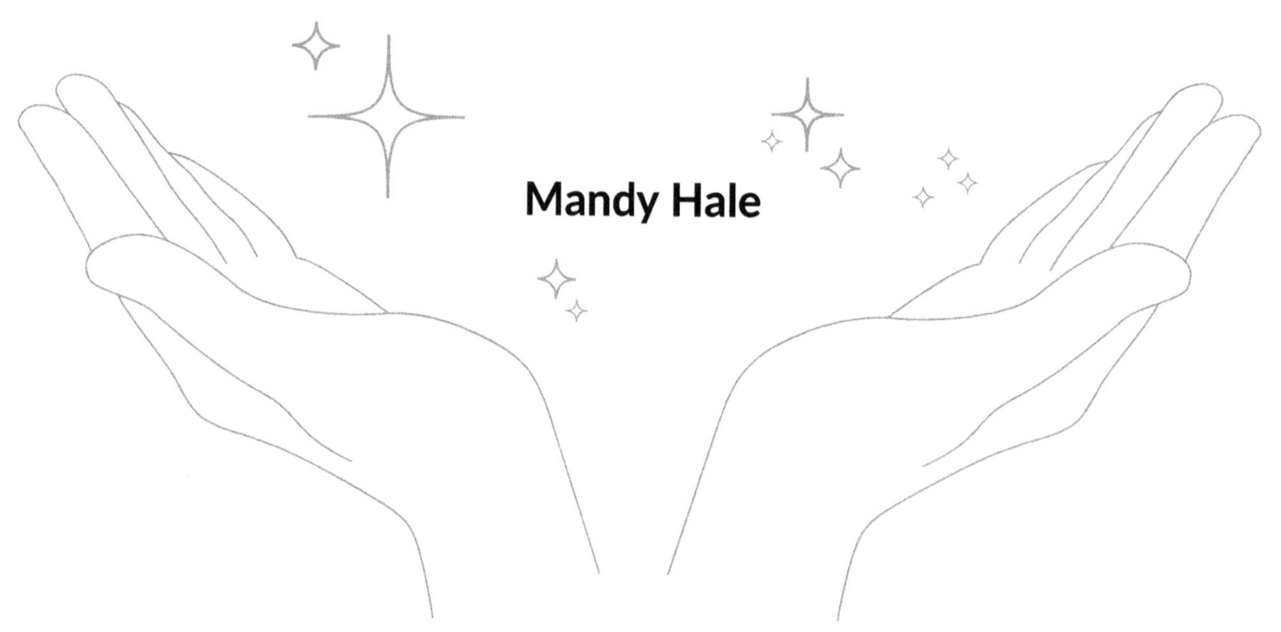

Look beyond surface-level desires and think about what truly serves you. Think of your life as a journey toward becoming your best self. What you want often represents comfort or instant gratification. What you need, however, might be more challenging or less appealing at first, but it leads to growth, wisdom, and fulfillment.

You have a big test coming up, you might want to binge-watch your favorite show because it's fun and easy. But what you need is to study and prepare.

When you focus on what you need instead of what you want, you're setting yourself up for long-term success and growth—even if it's not as fun in the moment!

My rating ☆ ☆ ☆ ☆ ☆

My thoughts:

"At the end of the day, it doesn't matter whether or not other people are comfortable with how you're living your life. What matters is whether you're comfortable with it"

Dr. Phil

Trying to please everyone can lead to stress and dissatisfaction because people will always have different opinions about how you should live. **What truly matters is whether your choices align with your values and bring you peace.**

Imagine wearing an outfit you love, but someone comments that it's "too bold" or doesn't suit you. If you change how you dress to make others happy, you will feel self-conscious and lose confidence.

But if you remind yourself that you feel good in it and that it reflects your style, their opinion won't matter as much.

My rating ☆ ☆ ☆ ☆ ☆

My thoughts:

"After a while, you learn
to ignore the names
people call you and just
trust who you are"

Shrek, 2001

Stop letting other people's opinions define your self-worth. Over time, you realize that what others say about you doesn't matter as much as what you believe about yourself. **True strength comes from trusting your values, abilities, and identity.**

Taylor Swift, in her early career, was criticized and called names for writing songs about her personal life. Instead of letting that define her, she trusted her talent and authenticity, continuing to write songs that resonated with millions. Today, she's one of the most successful artists in the world, proving that believing in yourself matters more than what others say.

My rating ☆ ☆ ☆ ☆ ☆

My thoughts:

"He who asks a question is a fool for five minutes; he who does not ask a question remains a fool forever"

Chinese Proverb

Remember Thomas Edison, the inventor of the light bulb? As a young boy, he was curious and often asked so many questions that his teachers thought he was "difficult." Despite being ridiculed, he kept asking questions and experimenting. His persistence and curiosity helped him create inventions that changed the world. Imagine if Edison had been too afraid to ask questions or explore his ideas because of what others thought?

Asking questions, even if they seem "foolish," is how we learn and grow. **It's far better to seek knowledge and face temporary discomfort than to miss out on opportunities for understanding and success.**

My rating ☆ ☆ ☆ ☆ ☆

My thoughts:

"When you get tired,
learn to rest, not quit"

Banksy

Take a break and nourish yourself when things get tough.
 When you're studying for a big exam and after a few hours, you start feeling mentally drained. Instead of pushing through and burning out, take a 15-20 minute break, grab a snack, or go for a walk (stay away from phone). When you return, you're more energized, focused, and you perform better.

It's normal to feel tired, but resting isn't giving up—it's making sure you're at your best for whatever comes next. You're setting yourself up for long-term success. It's all about knowing when to pause and recharge so you can perform at your best.

My rating ☆ ☆ ☆ ☆ ☆

My thoughts:

"I can accept failure, everyone fails at something. But I can't accept not trying"

Michael Jordan

Jordan is famous for being cut from his high school basketball team, a major early failure. Instead of accepting defeat and walking away, he used it as motivation to work harder. Over the course of his career, he missed more than 9,000 shots, lost nearly 300 games, and had 26 game-winning shots that didn't go in. Despite these setbacks, Jordan didn't let failure stop him; he kept trying, learning from each failure, and improving his game. His mentality helped him become a six-time NBA champion.

Jordan's message is clear: **failure doesn't define you. Not trying, however, means missing out on growth and achievement.**

My rating ☆ ☆ ☆ ☆ ☆

My thoughts:

"Let the improvement of
yourself keep you so
busy that you have no
time to criticize others"

Roy T. Bennett

Focus on improving yourself—whether it's your skills, mindset, or goals—you won't have time to judge or criticize other people. Direct your energy toward your own growth and development, rather than wasting it on negative thoughts about others.
Imagine you're on a school sports team, and a teammate is struggling to perform well. Instead of criticizing them, focus on your skills—practice harder, learn new techniques, and work on fitness. You'll have no time to criticize your teammate, and you might even be in a better position to help them improve.
Self-growth is a personal journey, and when you're committed to bettering yourself, you naturally become less concerned with the faults of others.

My rating ☆ ☆ ☆ ☆ ☆

My thoughts:

"Life shrinks or expands in proportion to one's courage"

Anaïs Nin

The size, richness, and depth of our experiences in life depend on the courage we display. **Courage allows us to step out of our comfort zones, take calculated risks, and embrace opportunities**, which leads to a fuller and more expansive life.

If we let fear dominate us, life feels smaller and more limited because we avoid challenges and growth.

If you summon the courage to try, you might discover talents you didn't know you had, make new friends, and grow more confident. Even if you don't win, the experience will teach you valuable lessons, making your life richer and broader.

My rating ☆ ☆ ☆ ☆ ☆

My thoughts:

"The pain of discipline is far less than that of no discipline"

Anonymous

Discipline means sticking to your commitments, even when it's hard. Like, waking up early to study for an important test might feel tiring and inconvenient. However, the reward of doing well in the test—and the doors it can open for your future—makes that effort worthwhile. And, if you procrastinate and skip studying, you might not do that well.

The regret and embarrassment that follow are far more painful than the temporary effort of being disciplined.

Discipline helps you stay focused and work toward your goals, while a lack of discipline leads to missed opportunities, setbacks, and the emotional pain of knowing you could have done better.

My rating 

My thoughts:

"The most painful thing
is losing yourself in the
process of loving
someone too much, and
forgetting that you are
special too"

Ernest Hemingway

When you deeply care for someone—be it a friend, a family member, or a partner—it's natural to want to make them happy. If you constantly put their needs above your own, sacrifice your interests, or change who you are to please them, you risk losing yourself. You might stop pursuing your hobbies, avoid hanging out with other friends, and even change your opinions to match theirs. At first, you might feel good because you're making them happy, but over time, you'll feel like you've lost a part of yourself. It can lead to feelings of emptiness.

A healthy relationship, whether with a friend, family member, or partner, is one where both people support each other while maintaining their individuality.

My rating ☆ ☆ ☆ ☆ ☆

My thoughts:

"I am a success today because I had a friend who believed in me and I didn't have the heart to let him down"

Abraham Lincoln

Encouragement of a supportive friend can inspire you to work harder and achieve success, even when you might doubt yourself.

Sometimes, you may not fully believe in your own abilities. **But when someone—like a friend, mentor, or teacher—believes in you, their trust can push you to strive harder and achieve things you didn't think were possible.**

It's their belief that becomes your strength, and you feel a sense of responsibility to not let them down.

My rating ☆ ☆ ☆ ☆ ☆

My thoughts:

"If you don't sacrifice for
what you want,
you will sacrifice
what you want"

Anonymous

Pursuing meaningful dreams or desires often requires effort, discipline, and giving up short-term comforts. If you're unwilling to make those sacrifices, you risk losing the very things you truly want in the long run. Say you want to excel in arts and get into a prestigious college. To achieve that, you need to sacrifice some things, like spending too much time on social media or skipping practice sessions for hangouts.

The choice is simple: sacrifice temporary pleasures for long-term rewards, or sacrifice your dreams because you didn't put in the effort when it mattered.

My rating ☆ ☆ ☆ ☆ ☆

My thoughts:

"If you don't know, the thing to do is not to get scared, but to learn"

Ayn Rand

Not knowing something isn't a failure—it's an opportunity to grow. Instead of being overwhelmed or discouraged, the best response is to seek knowledge and learn.

Life is full of situations where you might not know what to do, whether it's learning a new skill, or sorting out a tough situation with friends.

It's normal to feel unsure. Instead of panicking or giving up, take a step back and focus on finding answers. Learning gives you the confidence to face challenges.

My rating ☆ ☆ ☆ ☆ ☆

My thoughts:

"Holding on to anger is like grasping a hot coal with the intent of throwing it at someone else; you are the one who gets burned"

Buddha

When you harbor resentment or anger, it ultimately hurts you more than the person you are upset with. **Anger doesn't resolve problems; it only intensifies your pain and consumes your peace of mind.**

Say you're angry at a friend who said something hurtful. Instead of talking to them or letting it go, you hold onto that anger, replaying the moment in your head. While your friend may have moved on or might not even realize you're upset, your anger keeps bothering you. It distracts you from your studies, makes you irritable, and robs you of happiness. In the end, you're the one who suffers, not them.

My rating 

My thoughts:

"Those who sacrifice their principles for pleasure, soon lose both"

Anonymous

Compromising your values and principles for temporary enjoyment often leads to regret and the loss of both the pleasure and your sense of integrity.

Imagine you believe in honesty, but one day, you're tempted to cheat. You think, "It's just this once." If you're caught, you not only lose the pleasure of the win but also damage your trustworthiness. **Even if you're not caught, the guilt of going against your principles stays with you, making the "pleasure" hollow.**
Sticking to your principles is essential, even when temptations arise. True satisfaction comes from staying true to who you are and what you stand for.

My rating ☆ ☆ ☆ ☆ ☆

My thoughts:

"When you learn, teach;
when you get, give"

Maya Angelou

Share your knowledge and resources with others. Say you're part of a school project team, and you've learned a new technique to create a great presentation. Instead of keeping it to yourself to outshine others, you share it with your teammates, helping everyone succeed.

Life becomes meaningful when you share your growth and blessings with others. When you teach what you've learned and give what you've received, you not only help others but also create a cycle of kindness and empowerment that enriches everyone's lives—including your own.

My rating ☆ ☆ ☆ ☆ ☆

My thoughts:

"The past cannot be changed, forgotten, edited, or erased. It can only be accepted"

Anonymous

Everyone has moments they wish they could undo—failing a test, losing a friendship, or making a mistake. It's natural to feel regret, but no matter how much you think about it, the past won't change. Instead of wasting energy on what cannot be undone, focus on learning from those experiences and using them to make better choices in the future.

The past is like a closed book—you can read it, reflect on it, and learn from it, but you can't rewrite it. **Acceptance doesn't mean you approve of what happened; it means you're ready to let go of regret and focus on creating a better present and future.**

My rating ☆ ☆ ☆ ☆ ☆

My thoughts:

"It is hard to love yourself
if you never spend time
with yourself.
'Alone Time' is Necessary"

Izey Victoria Odiase

As a teenager, you might find yourself constantly surrounded by friends, family, and social media. While it's great to connect with others, it's just as important to spend time alone.

When you're constantly connected, and never take time to be by yourself, you might start feeling disconnected from your own emotions or lose touch with what truly makes you happy.

Taking time alone, like going for a walk or spending a quiet evening reading or painting gives you the space to check in with yourself, helping you feel more centered and confident in who you are.

My rating ☆ ☆ ☆ ☆ ☆

My thoughts:

"Take the attitude of a student, never be too big to ask questions"

Og Mandino

As we grow older or gain more knowledge, we might feel like we should know everything or that asking questions might make us seem "dumb." You might feel embarrassed to ask the teacher or your classmates for help, thinking that others will judge you. But when you ask questions, you're opening yourself up to learning something new.

Never let pride or fear hold you back from asking questions. Whether it's in school, in your personal life, or even in your future career, always maintain the mindset of a student— curious, open to feedback, and ready to learn. It's the key to personal and intellectual growth.

My rating ☆ ☆ ☆ ☆ ☆

My thoughts:

"You are what you do,
not what you say you'll do"

Carl Gustav Jung

It's easy to say, "I want to be a great student" or "I want to be healthier," but unless you take steps to follow through on those words, they remain just that—words. **Your actions reveal who you really are and what you truly care about.**

Don't just talk about what you want to do—show it through your actions. Consistency, effort, and dedication to your goals define who you are.

My rating ☆ ☆ ☆ ☆ ☆

My thoughts:

"However difficult life may seem, there is always something you can do and succeed at"

Stephen Hawking

You can feel overwhelmed when facing difficult situations like failing a test, dealing with personal struggles, or feeling like things aren't going the way you want.

Remember, success doesn't always look the same for everyone. It might not come in the form of perfect grades or winning every competition. **Sometimes, success is about making progress, learning from mistakes, or discovering something you're good at** that you didn't know before.

Keep going—you are capable of more than you realize!

My rating ☆ ☆ ☆ ☆ ☆

My thoughts:

"If you are annoyed by every rub, how will you be polished?"

Rumi

In life, you will encounter challenges, disagreements, and moments of frustration—whether it's in school, with friends, or even with your family. **These "rubs" or tough situations might feel uncomfortable, but they are opportunities for you to grow.**

If you avoid them or get upset at every challenge, you'll miss out on the lessons they bring. It's the discomfort of facing difficulties that helps you develop resilience, patience, and wisdom.

Don't shy away from the struggles or criticisms you face. They're part of your growth journey.

My rating   ☆ ☆ ☆ ☆ ☆

My thoughts:

"I'm not in this world to live up to your expectations and you're not in this world to live up to mine"

Bruce Lee

Everyone has their own path, dreams, and choices, and it's not fair to expect someone to conform entirely to our desires—just as we shouldn't feel pressured to meet others' expectations at the cost of our true selves.

Peer pressure often pushes you to act a certain way to gain acceptance, whether it's dressing a certain way, trying something risky, or agreeing with opinions you don't believe in. However, **living to meet others' expectations lead to unhappiness and a loss of your authentic self**. At the same time, you shouldn't expect your friends to always think or act like you do. True friendships respect individuality.

My rating ☆ ☆ ☆ ☆ ☆

My thoughts:

"It does not do
to dwell on dreams and
forget to live"

J.K. Rowling

Harry Potter and the Sorcerer's Stone

While dreaming is essential for envisioning a brighter future, focusing solely on dreams can lead to missing the beauty and opportunities in the present moment.

In relationships, whether it's with friends, family, or a romantic partner, it's easy to dream of everything being perfect—no arguments, full understanding, and constant happiness. But focusing too much on these fantasies can cause you to overlook the value of the real, imperfect bond you already have. **Relationships thrive when you live in the moment, communicate, and invest time and effort in the person you care about.**

My rating ☆ ☆ ☆ ☆ ☆

My thoughts:

Detangling Myself Activities

Quick Emotional Intelligence Self Assessment

Adapted from model by Paul Mohapel

Emotional intelligence (referred to as EI) is your ability to be aware of, understand and manage your emotions.

Take the assessment to learn your EQ strengths!

Rank each statement as follows:

0 (Never)

1 (Rarely)

2 (Sometimes)

3 (Often)

4 (Always)

1. Emotional Awareness

My Total Score _____________________

STATEMENT	SCORE
My feelings are clear to me at any given moment	0 1 2 3 4
Emotions play an important part in my life	0 1 2 3 4
I find it easy to put words to my feelings	0 1 2 3 4
My moods are easily affected by external events	0 1 2 3 4
I can easily sense when I'm going to be angry	0 1 2 3 4
I readily tell others my true feelings	0 1 2 3 4
I find it easy to describe my feelings	0 1 2 3 4
Even when I'm upset, I'm aware of what's happening to me	0 1 2 3 4
I am able to stand apart from my thoughts and feelings and examine them	0 1 2 3 4
My moods impact the people around me	0 1 2 3 4

2. Emotional Manangement

My Total Score ______________________________

STATEMENT	SCORE
I accept responsibility for my reactions	0 1 2 3 4
I find it easy to make goals and stick with them	0 1 2 3 4
I am an emotionally balanced person	0 1 2 3 4
I am a very patient person	0 1 2 3 4
I can accept critical comments from others without becoming angry	0 1 2 3 4
I maintain my composure, even during stressful times	0 1 2 3 4
If an issue does not affect me directly, I don't let it bother me	0 1 2 3 4
I can restrain myself when I feel anger towards someone	0 1 2 3 4
I control urges to overindulge in things that could damage my well being	0 1 2 3 4
I direct my energy into creative work or hobbies	0 1 2 3 4

3. Social Emotional Awareness

My Total Score _____________________________

STATEMENT	SCORE
I consider the impact of my decisions on other people	0 1 2 3 4
I can easily tell if the people around me are becoming annoyed	0 1 2 3 4
I sense it when a person's mood changes	0 1 2 3 4
I am able to be supportive when giving bad news to others	0 1 2 3 4
I am generally able to understand the way other people feel	0 1 2 3 4
My friends can tell me intimate things about themselves	0 1 2 3 4
It genuinely bothers me to see other people suffer	0 1 2 3 4
I usually know when to speak and when to be silent	0 1 2 3 4
I care what happens to other people	0 1 2 3 4
I understand when people's plans change	0 1 2 3 4

4. Relationship Management

My Total Score ________________________________

STATEMENT	SCORE
I am able to show affection	0 1 2 3 4
My relationships are safe places for me	0 1 2 3 4
I find it easy to share my deep feelings with others	0 1 2 3 4
Iam good at motivating others	0 1 2 3 4
I am a fairly cheerful person	0 1 2 3 4
It is easy for me to make friends	0 1 2 3 4
People tell me I am sociable and fun	0 1 2 3 4
I like helping people	0 1 2 3 4
Others can depend on me	0 1 2 3 4
I am able to talk someone down if they are very upset	0 1 2 3 4

My EQ strengths!

Mark your EQ total scores to assess your strengths and areas for improvement

Domain	Score
Emotional Awareness	0 2 4 6 8 10 12 14 16 18 20 22 24 26 28 30 32 34 36 38 40
Emotional Manangement	0 2 4 6 8 10 12 14 16 18 20 22 24 26 28 30 32 34 36 38 40
Social Emotional Awareness	0 2 4 6 8 10 12 14 16 18 20 22 24 26 28 30 32 34 36 38 40
Relationship Management	0 2 4 6 8 10 12 14 16 18 20 22 24 26 28 30 32 34 36 38 40

Measure your effectiveness in each domain using the following key:

00 - 24: Area for Enrichment: Requires attention and development

25 - 34: Effective Functioning: Consider strengthening

35 - 40: Enhanced Skills: Use as leverage to develop weaker areas

who
am
I?

Answer these reflective questions to get aware of who you are today. As you will grow and change, the answers to these questions might change as well. This could be a record of yor present version.

My favorite food is ...

My favorite music is ...

Important people in my life is ...

The talent or skill I'm most proud of is...

A hobby or activity I love doing is ...

The time of day I feel most energetic is ...

Something I dislike is ...

The place where I feel happiest is ...

An idea for my future I have is ...

If I could visit any place in the world, it would be ...

One thing I'm afraid of is ...

A movie, book, or show I enjoy is

When I feel stressed, I usually ...

Something I've done that made me proud is ...

If I could describe myself in one sentence, it would be

My Trust
Circle

Instruction

These circles represent different levels of trust and closeness:
1. **Inner Circle**: People you trust the most and feel closest to.
2. **Second Circle:** People you trust but not as much as those in the inner circle.
3. **Outer Circle:** People you know but don't trust fully yet.

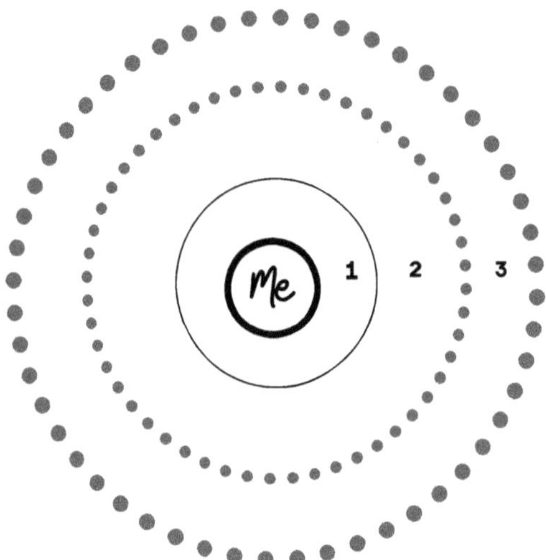

Now, think about the people in your life (family, friends, teachers, neighbors, etc.).
Write the names of the people you trust most in the inner circle.
Continue outward, writing names in the other circles based on the level of trust.

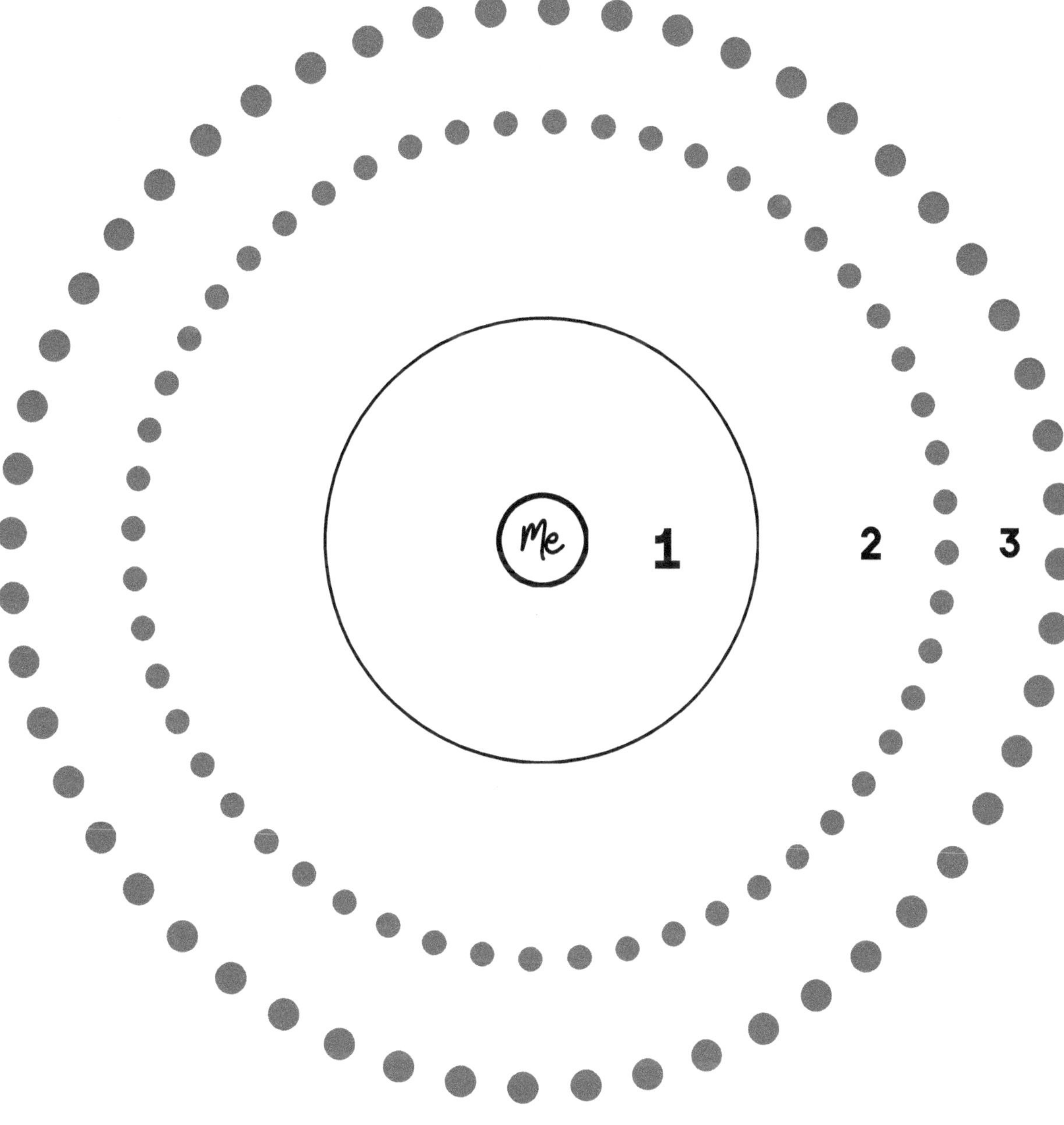

Me
1
2
3

Reflect

Think about these questions to understand yourself a little more.

1. What does trust mean to you?
2. How do you decide who belongs in each circle?
3. How can you show appreciation to the people in your inner circle?
4. What would someone need to do to earn more trust from you?
5. Why did you place certain people in specific circles?
6. How do thesee people make you feel safe or supported?
7. Are there people you'd like to move closer to the inner circle? If so, how can you strengthen those relationships?

•••

...

We are here to support you!

Life can feel overwhelming at times, whether it's about academics, performance, or personal challenges. Remember, you don't have to navigate these moments alone. At Habit Mantra, we believe in supporting you every step of the way.

If you ever feel stuck, need guidance, or just someone to talk to, we're here to help. No matter how big or small your concern is, reach out to us—you'll find a safe space, understanding, and encouragement to move forward.

Connect with Us
Feel free to email us at founders@habitmantra.com
Contact: 9934818582
Instagram @HabitMantra.

Your growth, well-being, and success matter to us. Together, we can tackle challenges, celebrate progress, and help you become the best version of yourself.

About Our Editor

Juhi Kumari is an alumna of the University of Sussex, where she earned her Master's in International Education and Development. She is also a Teach for India alumna and has extensive experience working with children in various roles, including teaching, curriculum development, and content management. As the founder of Habit Mantra, Juhi focuses on empowering students through career, performance, and life coaching. The organization utilizes scientific tools like psychometrics to guide students in their personal and academic development.

Hey there,
We sincerely hope you enjoyed reading this book.
Please scan the code and drop your precious review.